Prepare Your CPA Firm for a Sale

Brannon Poe, CPA

Prepare Your CPA Firm for a Sale

Independently Published

Copyright © 2023, Brannon Poe

Published in the United States of America

230113-02226.4

ISBN: 9798856709819

No parts of this publication may be reproduced without correct attribution to the author of this book.

Here's What's Inside…

Introduction 1

Chapter One
Planning- Why Bother? 7

Chapter Two
How Would a Buyer See My Firm? 10

Chapter Three
**What's the Current Market
Value of My Firm? 23**

Chapter Four
**What Is My Timing for Exit, and
What Are My Goals? 32**

Chapter Five
What Should I Stop Doing? 41

Chapter Six
Pricing Power 48

Chapter Seven
**How Do Unplugged Vacations
Help Me Build a Better Firm? 56**

Chapter Eight
Staffing and Delegation 62

Chapter Nine
**If You're on a Short Selling Timeframe,
What Do You Need to Focus On? 69**

Chapter Ten
Making Change Happen 72

Chapter Eleven
Here's How We Can Help You 77

**How to Prepare Your CPA
Firm for a Sale, Increasing the
Value and Freeing Up Your Time** 79

Introduction

Small changes made before an exit can have a major impact on the salability of your accounting practice. We wrote this book to empower firm owners with actionable strategies to help improve profitability, reduce owner dependence, and make their firms more attractive for an eventual sale.

These strategies also make firms easier and more enjoyable to own and operate while you still run the practice. A lot of the concepts in this book are taken from our practice management workshop, Accounting Practice Academy. APA was developed from years of accounting practice sales, mergers and acquisitions experience.

The practice management advice shared in this book helped Chris Hall, CPA, and Bill Murphy, CPA, add 25% to the market value of their CPA firm in about a year. They reduced owner hours and staff hours by selectively pruning their client list and improving team delegations.

Once they gained capacity, they implemented price increases and focused more partner time on their A-clients who needed more services.

These incredibly simple but powerful implementations increased their top-line revenues and net profit. The changes took a persistent effort, but once they had a clear vision of what needed to happen, they couldn't "unsee" that vision.

Most owners face too much to do and too little time for strategic planning. They are working "IN" their businesses instead of "ON" them. This book offers simple and practical steps that impact firm profitability and owner dependence. The hard part is changing old habits and actually implementing new ones.

Develop a crystal-clear vision for your practice, so you can tackle the changes you want to make. Once implemented, your firm will be more attractive to more potential buyers. This will make it faster to sell and at a higher multiple. You may even discover that your timetable for an exit gets extended because your ownership experience has been elevated.

You will work less and be more profitable. You will also improve your staff's working conditions, making attracting and retaining talent easier.

With all that spare time, you might even find time to remember why you went into business for yourself in the first place: Freedom!

To your strategic success,

Part 1
Perspective

"Life moves pretty fast. If you don't stop and look around once in a while, you could miss it."

— **Ferris Bueller**

Chapter One
Planning- Why Bother?

Planning, no matter how far ahead, is smart. The sooner, the better. Does it make a difference?

YES! It can have a major impact not only on the value of your firm but on your ownership experience leading up to your exit. Unfortunately, too many CPAs get caught up in the day-to-day. They work too many hours and focus on lower-level tasks at the expense of the important and impactful ones.

Planning with the end in mind gets owners focused on "the big stuff" that actually moves the needle. Well-managed firms sell faster and for premium prices. They also attract high-quality staff and buyers, and their owners work less, not more.

At Poe Group Advisors, we not only help people buy and sell firms, but we help owners build great practices too. There have been a number of occasions where owners have improved their firms and liked them enough to keep them longer. That's fine by us. We want you to sell when you are ready.

If you have a great firm, it will attract a lot of suitors. You'll have multiple options and the ability to transition out of your practice faster once the decision to exit has been made.

Build Your Vision - What's Your WHY?

What are your exit goals? Buyers do want to know a Seller's reason for exit. When do you want to exit? How long do you want to work after a transaction takes place? How long do you want to help with the transition?

When contemplating a sale, one of the first things we ask sellers is, "Why do you want to sell? What do you want to do with your time after you exit your business?" Some people have travel plans, or maybe they want to move to see grandchildren more. There can be some life events that are pulling them out of business.

People Only Change When They Have a Real Reason To Change.

We always advise our clients who begin thinking about a sale, "Spend some time thinking about that, envisioning what that next stage of life will look like for you. Find a vision or create one you can be excited about." That will be a big driver of change. When you have a why, then you will figure out the how and the when.

If you are not at the point of selling but want change, why? Do you need more time with your family? Are you feeling burned out? Identify it specifically. Again, create a vision of what you want. What do you want the firm to look like in 3 years? What about in 10 years? Don't be afraid to think big, and be sure to write it down.

Your Big Picture Vision is crucial to shaping the actions that will powerfully transform your firm and your schedule. Don't skip this step. Make the time to answer the questions above.

Chapter Two
How Would a Buyer See My Firm?

Looking at your business through the eyes of your buyer is a great perspective. When you put your house on the market, stage it, or start to clean it up, you think about things from that buyer's point of view. Your business is no different. If you have a traditional office, how does the office look when you walk in? Is it clean? Is it neat? Are your files organized?

Imagine for a moment that you are a buyer looking at the practice with fresh eyes. How do the financials look? How is the revenue growth? Does the cash flow to owner make this business enticing? This exercise forces you to create that bird's-eye perspective. This is a powerful motivator for you to make changes in your practice that would make it more desirable.

Zoom Out!

Look at your office and your firm culture. If someone walks into your office and sees shag carpeting from 1965 matched with old brown paneling on the wall, that may give them a moment of pause.

It's more than shag carpeting, though. It's everything, like the office's mood and décor. How does the staff get along?

It's the same with cloud firms. What does the tech stack look like? How is the data organized? How is the portal working? Are there strong internal systems and processes?

Collect Your Data

Whether you are looking towards selling, growing, or even cutting back, you have to know what your starting point is. My advice for what to track is to think of the data that a buyer might want to see and pull that together for yourself. Understand what your firm is worth as-is. Data is objective, even if it isn't always pretty.

When we sell a firm, we put together a document we call a practice profile. The confidential practice profile provides buyers with a complete high-level view of the firm. It includes important historical financial information like top-line revenue, P&L summaries, and owner cash flow. It also typically includes overviews of the tech stack, processes and systems, firm culture, staff longevity and capabilities, mix of services, a general description of the clients, and the industries served by the firm.

It also describes how the firm prices its services. Many buyers want to know if you charge by the hour or if you have implemented value pricing.

Most importantly, buyers want to see if the practice will meet their skillset and offer them reasonable work hours with enough money to live, grow and pay back their loans.

We find that when many owners initially assemble the data needed to complete the profile, they get incredible insight into their firms. Many are surprised at what they find out because they haven't been paying attention to such important drivers. They come away with a different perspective because they're often caught up in the day-to-day of it.

If you would like a comprehensive guide on the key drivers of firm value, please visit **poegroupadvisors.com/value**. *For a short list of valuation-related data points, please visit* **poegroupadvisors.com/snapshot**.

As mentioned, owner hours are very important to buyers. A lot of times, sellers don't even know how much they've been working because they don't record that. Owner hours are just one of the many possible Key Performance Indicators (KPIs) tracked by firm owners. Different owners maintain different KPIs.

Oftentimes, looking at KPIs gets put on the back burner, and seemingly more important client work gets prioritized. I highly encourage you to make the time to define and track your firm information. It will give you clarity on the clients that deserve your focus, the mix of services that you may need to rebalance, how you can optimize your working hours, and so much more. Knowledge is power, as the saying goes, and if you don't know where you are, you don't know where you are going.

> # Let's Paint a Picture –
> # The Ideal Situation:

Practice Is Not Owner-Centric.

As you approach the time to exit, the less the firm needs you, the more likely it will continue to work well for clients and staff, the more valuable it will be, and the more enjoyable your transition will be. If your firm is currently heavily dependent on the owner or owners, change does not come easy. Letting go can be very difficult. However, exiting is the ultimate letting go, so the sooner you start, the better.

Buyers and successors are increasingly interested in taking on a business that affords them the time to enjoy life. Ideally, the owners are working less than 2,000 total hours per year and can take several vacations per year where they are completely unplugged from all work.

Profitability Is Attractive.

Think about this from the buyer's perspective. They will have debt service to cover the acquisition. They will need a reasonable return for the risk taken, and they will want to earn an attractive amount for their time spent working. Granted, the importance of these factors will vary a great deal based on who the new owner is, but almost everyone can agree that the more profitable your firm is, the more desirable it is. For a <u>very</u> rough target, if cash flow to owner is equal to or greater than 50% of top-line revenue, that's generally considered to be attractive profitability for a small firm with a team of around ten or less. As firms get bigger, the owner cash flow does tend to decline because owner production as a percentage of the total declines.

Team and Culture Are Strong.

What is a strong team culture? It's one of those things that fall into the "know it when you see it" category, but it does have some measurable and/or observable characteristics, such as:

- Employee turnover is low.
- Staff members get along well together and are generally happy.
- Team members are constantly learning and advancing their skills.
- New, high-quality team members are consistently joining the firm, even though it's tough out there right now.

There Are No Competitive Threats or Other Major Obstacles for a Potential Buyer.

Firms may face a number of threats and obstacles. If there are major ones, you are probably well aware of what those are. Again, put yourself in the buyer's shoes and think about your practice from that vantage point. Some of the more common threats and obstacles we've seen are:

- Competitive threats from within. Do you have employees with significant client relationships who might leave and take clients or other team members with them? Planning tip: Make sure to have an assignable non-solicitation clause in your employment and contractor agreements. Assignability is very important.

- Overreliance on extremely large clients. Clients that represent over 10% of total revenues can be risky for a new owner.

- Partner friction. Partners who are not in agreement on when and how to exit or other operational issues contribute to strong animosity between partners.

- Mix of work challenges. Having a highly specialized focus area that few other CPAs have – or want to have— can shrink your pool of possible buyers or successors. An example would be expert witness revenue. Generally speaking, as firms get bigger, the challenges posed by the mix of work fade considerably.

Processes and Systems in Place Are Efficient and Well-Documented.

This is both self-explanatory and clear as to why this would be helpful to a successor. Your technology doesn't have to be state-of-the-art, but having systems and processes that are easy to follow and efficient to work with will be attractive to a buyer and will help to facilitate a smoother transition. File documentation also fits into this category.

Seller Is Clear About Future Plans and Timing.

Buyers will want to know. They will ask.

Possible options might include volunteering, CFO work, another business opportunity, or fulfilling a long-held retirement dream. Having plans tends to "pull" you out of the practice and provides incredible clarity around your timing.

Just Because You Tolerated It Doesn't Mean a New Owner Will

Being in business for years to decades, you get used to how things are. Often, you'll put up with things that a new owner would never tolerate. One of those is the number of hours that the owner works. I'm going to go ahead and apologize now for how much we'll be covering this topic. For those of you who work too much, you really need to read this. You know who you are.

CPA practices are traditionally very seasonal, with tax season hours being heavy. We've seen practices where owners work as many as 3,000 hours a year. There's a generational shift, and younger buyers, especially, are looking for more balance. They're looking for a business that will support their families and allow them to spend adequate time with them.

What Would Happen If You Started Working Less?

If your owner hours are too high for comfort, working on that will be **very** important to maximize the value of your firm. The good news is that this will also give you tremendous freedom and, believe it or not, probably more money, too.

One of the mindsets that is possibly the most counterintuitive for some of the CPAs we have worked with is the idea that time does NOT equal money.

Our observation has been that firm owners who've figured out how to manage their firms with a reasonable schedule have also been the most successful in terms of owner compensation. When you make time, it's easier to be strategic about making more money.

In the past, many CPAs had no choice but to work a lot of hours. The processes took longer, and they were in build mode and wanted to work on growing the business. Of course, they worked hard. It was more of the expectation of the time as well. And, to be fair, if you own a business, it's always good to be able to work long hours when necessary, but that doesn't have to be a constant.

Fast forward to today, and CPA firm owners don't have to work as much as they did 20 or 30 years ago.

We see a definite generational correlation between high owner hours with older owners. It's a mindset, and it's often a problem when it's time to exit.

We had a client we sold recently in the Southeastern U.S. who worked about 3,000 hours a year, and all sorts of problems were starting to appear in the practice. One, of course, was that the firm is very owner-centric. Another problem with high owner hours is there tends to be a correlation with higher employee turnover.

There's an acute staffing shortage in the CPA industry right now, and if the owner is expecting staff to work anywhere close to as hard as the owner's working, then that puts a lot of pressure on them. People want to work for an owner who's going to allow them to take time off and not work crazy hours as well, so it impacts the culture of the team.

We did sell that firm, but a lot of buyers told us that the hours were a deal-breaker.

A Key Point To Remember

Always remember perspective is very valuable, and if you don't like what you see, the sooner you realize it, the sooner you can alter the firm's trajectory. Even the best of firms have room for improvement.

Chapter Three
What's the Current Market Value of My Firm?

As mentioned in the previous chapter, knowing the value of your firm long before the time to sell is helpful. You'll be better able to assess your timing and the steps of improvement you want to take.

A common rule of thumb in the accounting industry is that sales price should equal one times the annual gross revenue. We see practices go for less than that, and practices go for much more than that. We look at several key factors to determine what that multiple should be. When you think about how much a practice is worth, remember the concept of the "**number of potential buyers.**"

For example, if you have 100 buyers who want your firm versus if you had two or three, what situation will produce the best deal for the seller? Of course, the more buyers, the better.

We Have Identified Several Key Factors That Impact CPA Practice Values

(Section co-written by Darryl Boyd, Regional Market Leader)

Location

This will have a very big impact on the number of potential buyers for a practice. In general, there are more buyers in large metropolitan areas and fewer buyers in remote, rural areas. When you sell a CPA practice, you are also "selling" the location. In our experience, some midsize metro areas will typically fetch a 10% premium, while others consistently attract enough buyers to justify a 20% premium. This is more likely in cities with more than two million in population. Desirable areas, such as growing metropolitan areas with high quality of life, can also help to attract more buyers. If these numbers seem vague, it is because there are so many location variables combined with practice variables. Valuation becomes as much of an art as it is a science.

Additionally, full-cloud firms are location agnostic, resulting in a much larger buyer pool.

Quite simply, when a seller can entertain multiple candidates interested in a practice, there is a greater likelihood of finding a purchaser who is a good fit and is willing to pay market value. If you own a virtual firm, please read our separate Cloud Firm Pricing Factors Report at **poegroupadvisors.com/resources**.

Size

In general, there are more buyers for practices that can be purchased and operated by a single owner. Practices under $2,000,000 generally fit into this category. Compared to larger practices, these firms are easier to manage, and it is easier for CPAs to qualify for acquisition financing for these amounts. As a side note, buyers of practices where revenue is greater than $2,000,000 per year are often even more focused on acquiring talented staff as part of the deal.

Marketing

Professionally marketed firms sell for higher multiples with cleaner terms. Owners who sell on their own not only limit their exposure to the full market but they also end up limiting discussions with a few purchasers at a time. Having an experienced intermediary who can guide sellers in selecting which buyers to spend time with and facilitate discussions in an efficient manner can help sellers maximize their time with prospects and engage more prospects. This maximizes the number of qualified buyers in the mix, as well as allows owners to maintain proper focus on the business while it is being marketed.

Profitability

The more profitable the practice, the higher the price. More buyers are certainly interested in highly profitable practices where average client fees are high. Higher fees equate to more money for less work. That being the case, profitability doesn't have the impact that many would think. This is primarily because many capable, experienced buyers are confident in their abilities to increase profitability once they take over. The profitability of a firm is usually quite malleable.

An important point for sellers to consider is that a buyer is not entering into the same situation as the seller is when leaving their practice. A seller, having made their money over the years, is often not as concerned with profitability and cash flow. They may even give their clients an inordinate amount of flexibility in taking time to pay. The buyer, however, has to service the acquisition debt. Lenders will take this into consideration when determining the loan amount, which can certainly impact the price of a firm. Even if the buyer is confident that they will be able to increase profitability, the lender bases their decision on the past, not the future. A more profitable practice means a larger loan and, therefore, more cash to the seller.

Mix of Services

Some buyers value a practice using a separate multiple for each line of service based on the desirability and potential for long-term profit. For example, a review engagement may have a multiple of 1.25 times, whereas a personal tax return may have a multiple of 0.8 times. Sellers tend not to like this method of valuation because it essentially says that a practice is worth the sum of the multiples of its mix of services. It is important to take the mix of services into account but also to consider the desirability and quality of high-value engagements.

Again, this is where the buyer pool is important. Different buyers value different things. For example, many CPAs would shun a bookkeeping practice, whereas bookkeeping practices are among the highest multiples of firms that we sell because they can be highly automated and operated with less experienced staff.

However, two general trends are becoming more common. Buyers tend not to want a practice with a high number of personal tax returns not connected with a business. There is also a growing number of buyers in the U.S. market who do not want audit work. These will reduce the buyer pool and may reduce the overall price.

Employees

Almost every conversation we've had lately with sellers or buyers has included the difficulty of finding staff. It used to be that it was hard to find good people; now, it's hard to find people at all. An experienced team of talented individuals is very valuable to a buyer. Employees also provide continuity for a practice transition. They become the buyer's team for succeeding in a practice. They are also the means by which a seller can delegate their own work so they can spend time on business development and working on the practice rather than in it.

Clients

Client quality has a huge impact on pricing. Not all clients are equal by a long shot. The most important considerations for evaluating client quality include:

- Fee quality
- Client churn rates
- Industry risk/volatility

- Complexity - (which impacts staffing requirements)
- Ease of doing business
- Size of clients (Large clients can pose higher retention risks)
- Age of clients

When we market firms, we create a detailed profile to provide buyers with a high-level understanding of the practice. Depending on the pertinent characteristics of the firm involved, we include as much information as possible to shed light on client characteristics.

For example, we often include a breakdown of clients by industry. Some industries are more risk-prone, while some are particularly desirable and even "Recession Proof" such as the medical industry. Buyers tend to want a wide range of industries to avoid any risk in a niche market. That said, some niche markets can be very desirable and profitable, especially when serviced remotely. Some buyers want to grow in a particular industry and will pay a premium to acquire firms with a concentration in that industry.

Another important factor for buyers is client size. Generally, larger clients pose more risk to the buyer even though they bring in a lot of revenue. Again, buyer perspectives differ greatly. This can be a plus to some and a deal-breaker for others.

Terms

There is an old saying, "You name the price, and I'll name the terms." Many private transactions involve lengthy earn-out periods. We believe that sellers have a tendency to take too much risk, and this is most often reflected in the terms. As mentioned above, terms that include earn-out structures generally net sellers less overall cash than clean break sales. Please read our blog, *Accounting Practice Sales Price and Terms*, for a more in-depth look at the relationship between price and terms.

Chapter Four
What Is My Timing for Exit, and What Are My Goals?

The most important decision CPA firm owners need to make when thinking about succession planning is when to bow out. It can be difficult, though, to know when to leave. Sometimes an outside event brings clarity: health problems, a spouse's retirement, or the arrival of grandchildren.

But, in the absence of these major life events, owners need to decide when to exit without any outside influence. There are downsides to exiting either too soon or too late.

Risks of CPA Firm Succession Too Soon

If the succession is too soon, the owner may find letting go of the practice difficult or even impossible. Exiting owners who are not ready to let go often end up micromanaging their successors, which damages the handoff. When owners have no concrete plans to pull them out of the practice, they may unknowingly sabotage their own transactions. Deals can suffer from "death by a thousand cuts" as they go through multiple rounds of changes and become needlessly complex.

Risks of CPA Firm Succession Too Late

Too late, and owners can experience burnout. Their energy for the business can gradually fade to the point where the practice isn't growing or improving. Or, worse, the practice can go into decline as the clients and staff begin to leave.

There are a few factors to consider that can help you achieve the "Goldilocks zone" of timing.

Factors To Consider for Timing of CPA Succession

Money for Retirement

This is often the biggest consideration. CPAs are usually financially savvy and know when they have enough money to retire. That said, they should still take conservative projections of future earnings into account.

Post-Retirement Plan

Ideally, know what you want to do after your exit and have something in mind that you are drawn toward, such as volunteering, CFO work, another business opportunity, or fulfilling a long-held retirement dream. Having plans tends to "pull" you out of the practice and provides incredible clarity around your timing. It's much easier to leave your career when there are other things that you really want to do.

If you're not sure what you'll do, consider part-time work. Surprisingly, in our experience, many CPAs underestimate their ability to find lucrative part-time opportunities outside of public accounting. A lengthy career in public practice can provide a variety of skills and wisdom that have significant value, which can lead to CFO roles and general business opportunities. These roles often let exiting owners work less without sacrificing all of their income. This option offers a nice step-down in responsibility and time commitment, along with significant earning potential.

Total Transition Time

The length of the exit period will vary significantly from owner to owner and is influenced by many factors. If your partner agreement includes an exit plan, then congratulations on the good planning! If not, initiate a partner discussion on this issue so you can draft an addendum to your agreement. Regardless of your agreement, the sooner you begin a conversation with all partners about your exit, the better. Partners often have significantly different exit timetables, which can create conflicting interests. Identify any conflicts early, and solutions will be much easier to create.

Things To Consider for CPA Firm Transition Time

These are some of the most common considerations when determining your transition out of your CPA firm and handoff to the new owner.

Partnership or Shareholder Agreements

Ideally, your agreements will specify a clear path for exiting. Unfortunately, we've seen cases where firms did not have partnership agreements, or these agreements did not address exit or buyout concerns. (In fact, an AICPA firm succession management survey found that only 63% of firms have a partner agreement.) In some of these instances, the lack of a prior agreement delayed the exit timetable of the partner who wanted to leave. Legal conflicts can take years to resolve.

Client Transition Needs

The time necessary to facilitate a successful client transition can vary quite a bit. Some transitions last a few weeks, while others occur over a couple of years. Our general recommendation is to transition very quickly when a practice is sold. Though it may seem counterintuitive, our experience has been that firms overwhelmingly do better when the handoff is swift.

The topic of client transition is very complex. To better understand how long your transition may take, please explore our blog on high-level concepts behind successful transitions- *Tips for a Successful Accounting Practice Transition*.

Preparing Your Successor Takes Time

Even if you've chosen a successor, be sure to be objective about all of the necessary capabilities that ownership requires. Make a realistic assessment of their skills and weaknesses. Also, be sure they have a strong desire to take over. We've seen owners spend years grooming successors only to learn that they don't want the responsibility or aren't willing to pay a reasonable price for the practice.

No matter which route you choose as your exit, our experiences have shown us that CPA practice owners that have clear goals for what they want to do after the exit are the happiest.

Part 2 Actionable Strategies

"Action speaks louder than words but not nearly as often."

— **Mark Twain**

Chapter Five
What Should I Stop Doing?

Capacity is a big challenge for a lot of firm owners, especially in light of current staffing shortages in the accounting profession. It's harder and harder for owners to get and grow their teams. Capacity, therefore, is sometimes hard to find in a CPA firm. We've noticed that if you're trying to embark upon any firm improvement, the first place you need to start is to try to create some capacity. Now, that could mean hiring people. If you can find good people, that's certainly an ideal way to create owner free time, but there are also many other ways. In many cases, it's better to first look at these other strategies before hiring.

Returning to what we discussed in part one, taking stock of what you're currently doing regarding the mix of services is usually the best place to start. An insightful exercise for the firms we coach is to analyze all of the segments of their practice. Over the years, several firms have realized that one or more segments were either breaking even, at best or, often, losing money. For firms dabbling in anything, that's usually an opportunity to eliminate a segment.

Generally, less than 15 team members would qualify as a small firm. Our observation for small firms in the U.S. market that perform only a few audits per year has generally been that they're losing money on those audits. If they eliminate that segment, they have capacity immediately, as well as eliminating a source of loss. That newfound capacity can be refilled with higher level, better work that's more in keeping with the other offerings that are profitable and where the firm has more capability to add value for clients. As a bonus, team members are often relieved that they no longer have the intellectual burden of keeping up to date on both audit standards and tax law. (For various reasons, this is not always the case for audit work in Canada.)

Another way to capture more time is by hiring administrative help. You don't necessarily need professional staff to add capacity. We've often seen firms succeed in bringing on administrative personnel, which is a little easier to find. By working with their team, they have found ways to delegate duties from the professional staff to the administrative staff. That can also free up a lot of capacity.

Let Clients Go

Another way to do it is to let clients go. Many of the firms we've worked with have some smaller clients. When they look at the profitability of those smaller clients, they realize that many of those clients, for one reason or another, are not profitable. Unfortunately, this can be true of large clients too.

Sometimes, the biggest client can be the biggest problem. They are not only a drain on time but on morale. Take a look at the hours of time spent on all of your clients and see who can be better served at another firm. Letting clients go can be a wonderful source of capacity. We have a "letting clients go letter" on our Accounting Practice Academy website. Download your free copy at the resources page of **AccountingPracticeAcademy.com.**

The Half Tax, Half Audit Firm Story

Years ago, we had a firm that sold off a portion of its practice. They were about half tax and half audit. The audit side found that it was harder to find high-level staff. They decided a specialized practice in just tax would prove efficient and more lucrative.

They successfully sold off the audit segment of their practice. The practice grew to its original size within two to three years as a 100% tax-centered practice. Not only did they regrow their practice very quickly, but their cash flow increased substantially.

Orphan Personal Tax Returns

Another place for people to analyze their client list is to look at their tax returns that are not associated with a business. We call those orphan personal tax returns. Unless you're doing a lot of those efficiently and pricing them appropriately, those can be a big drag on the practice.

We did an analysis of our deals recently. We looked at firms that spent the most time on the market or didn't sell and compared those to firms that sold in a reasonable time frame. We noticed a very high correlation between firms with too many personal tax returns sitting longer or not selling compared to other firms.

Another trend we noticed with those firms is that, more often than not, they had less cash flow to owner and more staff turnover. Of course, there were exceptions, but in general, firms with a high number of orphan personal tax returns did not perform as well as those with fewer. If you think about it, when you have a lot of personal tax returns during tax season, you will have to staff up to handle that volume. That means you might have staff who aren't fully utilized in the other parts of the year, or your tax staff work a lot of hours during tax season. In a tight labor market, overworking your staff is not an attractive employee retention strategy. We have seen that buyers are increasingly staying away from firms with too many personal tax returns.

Automate Your Processes

Automation and systems improvement could be another category to pick up time and create capacity. However, those don't usually create the immediate time savings people hope for. They don't move the needle quickly. If you're at capacity, making systems changes usually requires an investment of time to focus on implementations and training staff. The learning curve with new technology and new processes may slow your people down initially before you see any benefit. On the other hand, if you fire a client, you immediately get time.

Automation is a great selling feature, however. I do suggest that as you gain capacity, you invest your freed-up time in great technology. This will net you more profit when it comes time to sell and often simplifies processes in the long run.

Grow While Vacationing

We had an Accounting Practice Academy™ member, Greg Toner, who implemented many of these strategies. He let go of some personal tax clients, did a great job delegating, and went from about two weeks of vacation to eight weeks per year while growing his firm.

How To Start Taking Action

It doesn't need to be hard to take action. Make it easy by making it so. The important thing is to start!

The common mindset of **"more is better"** is a hard concept to shake. It might feel odd to start thinking, "Oh, I want to grow my firm. What can I cut?" It feels counterintuitive and strange. I suggest starting by letting one client go or letting one task go to someone else. Starting slowly is better than not starting at all. Initiating some action steps will get you going down that path to freedom and growth.

Chapter Six
Pricing Power

Often, we'll hear CPAs tell their clients, "Hey, I've got people to pay. I have to raise my prices." It's not entirely inaccurate. Fewer people are coming into the profession, and more are leaving the profession, so there is a diminishing number of professional staff in the industry, creating shortages.

CPA firms in many markets are not taking new clients right now because they don't have the capacity. When you have an imbalance of supply and demand, you have price increases. That's how markets work. I don't think that it's a bad thing that CPA firms are raising their prices.

For entry-level accounting students and graduates, there's a 150-hour rule in the United States to become a CPA, which is essentially a master's degree. The starting salaries are not currently as competitive as other related professions, so students are not choosing to pursue accounting degrees. Entry-level salaries are a powerful signal for more people to go to school and graduate in a particular field, so it is a positive occurrence that prices are going up in the profession. Those higher prices provide the cash flow that most firms need to pay the higher salaries demanded in a tight labor market.

Honestly, if you own a firm and you're not analyzing your pricing, you're probably making a big mistake. I've never seen this level of imbalance in the marketplace, and we've been selling firms since 2003. Every day, we speak with firm owners, and most tell us they are unable to find new staff, and it's hard to keep the people they have. They have to pay more to keep existing employees and attract new staff.

Our Accounting Practice Academy™ members do a lot of experimentation with pricing.

In terms of losing clients, they're finding that it doesn't have the effect they think it will when they increase pricing. A lot of accountants are cost-conscious themselves. They consider themselves a bit price-sensitive and assume their clients are equally as price-sensitive. These experiments with raising fees have shown us that clients are very service-sensitive. They want their work done well, and they want key insights and advice. **Clients are service-sensitive, not price-sensitive.**

We've seen that when our APA members have increased prices, sometimes 20 and 30% across the board, they lose a small fraction of their total clients. They're not getting much pushback from clients, far less than they thought they would. One member doubled prices and lost only 7% of his client base. He essentially doubled his revenue while decreasing his number of clients and adding capacity. I'm not recommending that everyone go out and double their fees, but I suggest that owners experiment to see what their particular market will accept.

Experimenting Is the Key

Experiment with new clients who are coming in for new services. If you're not losing at least 50% of your proposals, you're probably not anywhere close to being priced correctly. Your prices are likely significantly lower than what the market will bear.

Create an experimentation process. Every market is different, and each firm's services are at least a little different. I don't recommend a one-size-fits-all pricing approach. It's very much a process of trial and error. I often recommend that firm owners increase fees on clients they are considering firing. If you've identified some clients you don't want to keep because you don't earn enough from them, try a price increase instead of firing them. See how much higher your prices have to be before they decide to leave the firm.

However, raising prices isn't always an effective method for pruning your client base. We've seen many firm owners attempting to prune their practices with price increases. They raise prices, thinking this will result in less volume, but they don't lose very many clients. They realize they might have to terminate some engagements if they truly need to prune.

Remember, raising the price makes a sweeter relationship out of a sour one; for you, anyway.

Value Pricing vs. By the Hour

We are huge proponents of value pricing. We have seen that firms with clients on fixed-price packages are very desirable in the marketplace. For instance, maybe you have a business client for whom you're doing monthly bookkeeping, quarterly advisory, year-end tax planning, and year-end tax preparation. You could bundle that into an annual or monthly fee.

If you go one better, set the fee up as an automatic ACH payment or a credit card payment, so there's no billing effort involved in the practice. That's the model that we recommend. It's not easy to transition from a traditional hourly billing model to a value pricing model, but it's a worthwhile change.

Another option is to offer different levels of service and different packages. This is something that Ron Baker, an industry thought leader around pricing, recommends. You can have a silver, a gold, and a platinum package, for example. Maybe the gold package has tax planning, but the platinum adds on advisory.

You have different levels of pricing, and people can choose. It's a way to, for lack of a better word, upsell. The clients like it because it's financially predictable, and they know what service to expect from you. You might be surprised by how many clients want more from you and are willing to pay for it. If you are creating more value for them, why wouldn't they?

How Do You Go From Hourly To Value Pricing?

Forget the "effort equals time equals money" formula. That's a mindset that keeps you trapped in a certain system. It's very limiting. You must shift your perspective to look at it from the client's point of view: "How does the client value it?" The truth is different clients are going to value your services very differently.

For instance, tax planning could mean hundreds of thousands of dollars of tax savings for a wealthy client. Is your hour spent on that client worth the same as if you were doing tax planning for a young couple with only wage income who just bought their first house? Tax planning is going to have a different dollar value for each of those clients. The wealthier client will pay more. You might have to research and spend more time on those planning strategies, but those ideas will have more value.

You have to shift to thinking more carefully about what value each service brings to your clients. An interesting thing happens when you start to think that way. You start to think, "Well, what do my clients value?" You might realize, "I think I can add value to this client by offering advisory services, and I think I can help that person grow their business. I could help this other client improve their business by going through a simple quarterly meeting rhythm. What would they be willing to pay for that?"

Again, it goes back to experimentation, but imagine that shift away from, "Well, how long will this take me?" That's a very different question than, "What's going to be most valuable to the client?"

Where To Start

Keep it simple! Where can you experiment without much risk? You could experiment with new clients and with clients who wouldn't have much impact on your practice if you lost them. That would be my suggestion. If you want to start, start experimenting where the risk is low.

Chapter Seven
How Do Unplugged Vacations Help Me Build a Better Firm?

In this chapter, we will dive into how a prospective buyer determines whether your firm is owner-dependent. If your firm is highly owner-dependent, taking a completely unplugged vacation would be much more difficult.

Also, it's not uncommon for people to start wanting to think about selling when they're getting burned out. Vacations can help with rejuvenation – assuming you're not working while you're on vacation! This means cutting yourself off entirely from the office. Yes, that's right, go cold turkey. No calling the office every day and no checking emails. It means truly unplugging.

Taking a long vacation means you have to prepare for it ahead of time, and you have to work a little harder when you get back.

Preparation is a forcing mechanism that requires you to delegate work. Your team will have to handle things while you're away. The increased amount of delegation is a major benefit. It's a way to practice letting go and letting the firm run without the owner.

Unplugged Means Unplugged

No cheating. You can't be on vacation and wonder if that one client got all the paperwork they were waiting on. One email can suck you right back into the office. It typically takes a couple of days to detach and be able to forget what's happening back at work.

If you want some good guardrails, don't take your cell phone. Please don't take your computer because having that available prompts you to think more about what's happening back in the office.

If you know you don't have an easy way to check in, then your brain's more likely to turn its attention to what you should be focusing on – your vacation, your family, and wherever you are.

The key to successful unplugging is to not let your clients have your personal cell phone number, if at all possible.

How To Prepare for Your Unplugged Vacation

Three to four weeks before a long vacation, I let clients know that I'm going to be gone and that I'll be unavailable. A lot of times, if work needs to happen soon, it can prompt new work to come in. Often, that will prompt clients to say, "Oh, well, I'm glad you let me know. I've got this project I need you to look at." It can expedite getting work in.

Then the same thing applies to your team. You let them know you're going and brief them on your expectations while you're gone. Someone has to look after your email. Someone has to look after your phone messages. I encourage my team to take a stab. If they're not sure how to handle a situation, do the best they can. If there are problems, they'll still be there when I return. I don't need to know about them when I'm in the middle of my vacation.

Many times, something that seems crazy at the moment will usually work itself out when given a little time to sit. Your team can figure it out. It is very empowering for your employees to think for themselves.

How I Discovered the Unplugged Vacation

We had a client in Canada years ago. He informed me that he was going on a three-week vacation and would not check his email. I asked him, "How do you do that?" He said, "Well, the first time I did it, I wondered when I was in the airplane looking down at my city if I was going to have a business when I came back."

His advice was to just do it. You have to let go and trust that everything will be all right. He told me they do that every year. He and his wife pick out some place interesting where they want to travel. They've been to Egypt. They've been all over Europe. In fact, they've been all over the world.

That gives him something to look forward to every year. Working hard during tax season made it worthwhile because he knew a trip was on the horizon. It brought him closer to his wife, and his staff stepped up. This was a very successful client. He had very good cash flow to owner.

Another surprising thing was that clients were not upset that he was taking time off. They were excited for him. They wanted to hear about his trip. They wanted to hear about his travels and where he would go next. Rather than it being a wedge in the client relationships, it was something that they took an interest in. He found that it helped his relationships.

Start Now

The best way to start your unplugged vacation is to go right now and find a time on your calendar when you think your workload is most conducive to taking a significant trip. Then book your trip. Buy your plane tickets and block the time from your calendar so you're committed.

Keep it simple and commit to not taking a computer or a way to check email.

For a deeper dive into this topic, go to **poegroupadvisors.com/unplugged**

Chapter Eight
Staffing and Delegation

This is the perfect next step when discussing an unplugged vacation. We talked earlier in the book about industry staffing constraints.

It takes time to invest in the proper delegation of tasks. If done well, that investment of time will help not only the owner but also the team members who find relief as things can come off their plates.

We have what we call the 3-Bucket Tool. You can download this simple tool on our website at **AccountingPracticeAcademy.com**. We essentially have you divide your duties into three buckets. One bucket is "keep." The second bucket is "delegate one day," and the third is "delegate now." You could even add a fourth column that says, "Things that you want to add to your plate." That's good for team members.

We've had some APA members bring this worksheet to a conference room, sit around the table, put 10 to 20 minutes on a timer, and have everyone fill it out. Then, they share what they want to let go of and what they want to keep. If you've added the fourth column – the things you want to add – that can be a powerful exercise to discover what team members see as an opportunity for growth.

For example, you might find that somebody on your team wants to do tax review work. They want to become a reviewer. Well, that might be the same thing that the owner wants to delegate. It's such a simple exercise to go through. Poll the team on what they're working on and find ways to reshuffle within the team so that everyone gets more of the things they do better and faster than other team members and fewer of the things they don't enjoy.

Dan Sullivan, the founder of Strategic Coach, created a concept he calls Unique Ability®, and that's what's at play here. Learn more at uniqueability.com.

Our 3-Bucket Tool will also highlight things that often can be handled by administrative staff. Many tasks that the professional staff want to get off their plates can often be handled by staff that is easier to hire or can even be outsourced. On our team recently, we've hired a couple of virtual administrative assistants, which has been a huge help for our team.

The other thing that can help with staffing is remote working. Having remote capability and entertaining the idea of staff working either in a hybrid mode or entirely from home is a competitive advantage in today's marketplace. Some professional staff won't want to work from home, but others will want to work only from home. Plus, the number of potential staff members increases drastically when your geography is unlimited. Offering remote options can also help with staff retention.

As an example, we had a client last year out of Austin, Texas. He had two remote tax preparers, one in California and one in the Northeast. Remote firms are not limited by geography for potential workers – or potential clients.

You can hire the best person for the position, no matter where they live. Remote capabilities can also make your firm more marketable, as the next case study demonstrates.

The Small Town USA Story

We sold a firm for a CPA named Barbara Agerton. She operated in a small town in California. Her husband's job moved to Texas, and so she decided to create a virtual firm. She transitioned her traditional practice into a cloud firm where she lived in Texas and operated the firm from there. Visit our cloud resources page at **poegroupadvisors.com/cloud-resources** for useful resources for building a profitable and scalable cloud accounting firm.

When she decided to sell her practice, it was much more marketable. If we had sold it as a traditional practice in a small town in California, a very rural town with a fairly low population, it would not have been easy to find a buyer in a reasonable amount of time. In the market for rural practices, the number of buyers tends to be lower than if you're in a major metropolitan area or if you have a virtual firm. When she sold her practice, she got more than she thought she could, and it sold within a few months, a very quick and lucrative sale for her.

Part 3 Implementing

"If you do not change direction, you may end up where you are heading."

— Lao Tzu

Chapter Nine
If You're on a Short Selling Timeframe, What Do You Need to Focus On?

Often, for whatever reason, people find themselves needing to sell quickly, and they wonder, "What can I do to spruce up the practice to make it as favorable as possible?" I put these things in the category of curb appeal. There are quick things that you can do to help your firm present better to a buyer.

It goes back to the ideas I discussed in Chapter Two: How would a buyer see your firm? If you have a traditional office, is it clean? If you walk into the owner's office, are there piles of paper everywhere, or does it look pretty tidy? Buyers want to buy a practice that's easy to operate. The systems need to be easy to understand. The records should be easy to follow. The work papers from one year to the next must be consistent, and there should be an easy system to replicate and review the work and understand the files.

All those things are important, and any cosmetic issues do make an impression on a potential buyer. Take a look at your practice from a buyer's perspective. Does it need a fresh coat of paint or a deep cleaning? What's the condition of the carpeting? Fixing these issues should be your first priority.

How Do Your Numbers Look?

Another important factor involves the numbers. Do what you can with the time that you have to make the practice look good on paper. Many practitioners have old accounts receivables. Not that buyers are buying the accounts receivables, but if there are a lot of slow-paying clients, that doesn't look good. Do what you can to clean that up. Slow-paying clients could mean no-paying clients, and a buyer wants reliable income. Trying to collect old receivables is always helpful.

Some systems changes can be relatively easily implemented. If you're almost paperless, you can go ahead and finish the transition and become fully paperless. If you still have a server but also use a couple of applications, you could easily switch to the cloud and eliminate the server. That shift is attractive. No one wants a server with an uncertain and unpredictable lifespan. Even if you're mostly virtual, some simple changes can have a big impact.

We recently spoke with a client who had a small-town practice. She had almost completely turned her firm into a virtual one, but some things were still in the traditional mode. She was still meeting with a handful of clients in person. I encouraged her to go ahead and make her firm fully virtual. This small change will help get the practice sold much quicker, especially in a small town.

My Encouragement to You

Again, look at your practice through the buyer's eyes. It may be helpful to ask a friend or colleague to come by your office and give their impressions or do a walkthrough. It's amazing how that stack of papers in the corner you've blocked out of your mind can be a problem, and someone else can spot it right away.

Chapter Ten
Making Change Happen

Start Ugly and Keep It Simple

Change is always a little messy. You have to accept that. Starting is more important than being perfect. If you wait and think through every little possibility or every reason not to do something, you'll find several. There's a real risk that you won't do anything and will go right back to your old habits.

One thing that many people can identify with is the challenge of changing health habits. When you're trying to eat healthier, exercise, or lose weight, it's easy to fall back into old habits. That's human nature. To combat the pull to stick with old habits, we find that it's very important to know your why. What is your vision? Why do you want to change? Maybe you're trying to sell for a certain price or sell by a certain time.

Maybe you're feeling burned out and can't afford to stop working, but you know you need to change.

This goes back to Chapter One. Whenever you are preparing for a major change, it is important to identify your why and connect with it on a very emotional level. Make it real, and with that, create a vision. Make that vision as clear and vivid as you can. The clearer and the more vivid you can make that vision, the better. If you have a powerful vision of where you want to go, that's a big step toward making a change because you're highly motivated to make it a reality.

I recommend putting the goal and vision to paper. Writing it down can have a profound effect on your success in seeing the vision through. Ask yourself, with each new client or proposed shift in the business, "Does this move me towards my practice vision?" That lens can help keep you focused on the right work.

We've been coaching accounting firm owners for quite some time and have found that if they have a strong reason to change, they will.

Selling is a big event. It's a big life shift, and that strong vision is very helpful.

Win Early and Win Often

The other thing is to get some early wins. Find the easy wins. Whether creating some capacity by letting some clients go or playing around with price increases on new clients, find the easiest few things you can change, and then take action. We've found that people who do this early tend to build momentum.

You want to start seeing results. Having tangible results is a very big motivator to get more. This is why tracking KPIs is so important. You need to be able to see the changes clearly.

The truth is that growth and relief are possible. We know it's possible because we've seen many of our clients build practices that serve them in ways that many accountants can't even imagine.

We sold a client's practice about a year ago in Canada. This firm owner had other businesses. He had one business that was probably four times the size of his accounting practice. He set up his accounting practice so that he worked about 500 hours a year in total, and his cash flow to owner was still extremely strong. It was a very profitable practice.

He could have made a great living from the accounting practice alone, but he had these other businesses. His opportunity cost was high, so he couldn't work full-time in the practice. He had an amazing team. He treated them extremely well and kept them for a long time. His practice was not owner-dependent. He only had great clients, and it was a very easy practice to sell. All of these things are possible if you put your mind to them. His constraints forced him to find solutions.

We all have these natural barriers that prevent us from making change. Whether it's your mind finding all the reasons not to do something and dwelling on those risks or a lack of staying power, we call them FTIs, failures to implement. You can have these great ideas and a grand vision and still have some natural FTIs.

Take stock and look at how you've changed in the past. What have you done that worked? If you were trying to lose weight, was it getting accountability that made the difference? Was it getting people in a weight loss contest? Did you empty out your cabinets and put all new food in there? What was it? When you've failed in the past, why have you failed?

Be creative in leveraging these ideas that helped you make changes in the past. Taking stock of your natural successes and your failures in the past can help you create a strategy that's more likely to work in changing your practice.

Chapter Eleven
Here's How We Can Help You

The first question we ask a potential client is, "What's your timeframe?" It's the biggest decision someone has to make when they're exiting. It can also be one of the hardest decisions you have to make. Depending on the answer, that will create a very different conversation. If someone has a longer timeframe for sale, we're happy to help them understand their practice a little bit better, how a buyer will see that practice, and what it's worth now so they can start that planning process.

If you're a more immediate seller, we can look at your firm and give you an outside perspective on what the market would look like and some short-term things you might be able to do if you want to implement any changes before going on the market.

Our Hope for You

We hope you will plan sooner and that you have been inspired to take action toward a more profitable, smoother exit.

The best way to find us is to go to our website, where we have a vast library of free resources. Go to **poegroupadvisors.com** and register as a seller.

Look at our coaching program, **accountingpracticeacademy.com**, and see if you want to enroll.

How To Prepare Your CPA Firm for a Sale, Increasing the Value and Freeing Up Your Time

You've done a great job building your CPA firm over the years. Are you wondering what your firm is worth and if you can increase its value before you sell?

That's why we wrote this book. Every day, we help people like you increase their firms' value before they sell. Spend less time working "in" the business and enjoy the perks of "owning" the business instead of the business owning you.

To learn more about the ideas discussed in this book, go to **poegroupadvisors.com** and follow these three steps:

Step 1: Download your **Valuation Key Factors Report** to take a deeper dive into what drives accounting practice values.
poegroupadvisors.com/value

Step 2: Download the **Practice Value Questionnaire** for a tailored valuation estimate created specifically for your firm.
poegroupadvisors.com/snapshot

Step 3: Call us at **888-246-0974** to discuss your particular circumstances, whether you are ready to sell now or years from now.

"We look forward to helping you grow and eventually sell your firm for the best price and terms possible."

Made in the USA
Columbia, SC
25 June 2025